Lake Superior

Great Lakes of North America

Harry Beckett

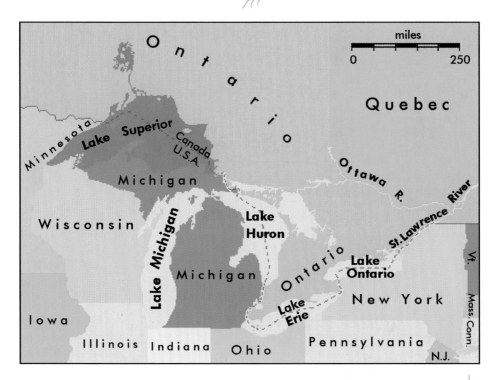

The Rourke Corporation, Inc.
Vero Beach, Florida 32964

PHOTO CREDITS:
Photographs by kind permission of: Geovisuals, Waterloo, Ontario; National Archives of Canada; Rapid Magazine, Scott McGregor; Duluth Convention and Visitors Bureau; Michigan Travel Bureau; Michigan Sea Grant; Maps by J. David Knox; Ontario Archives; Rapid Magazine, Scott MacGregor; Great Lakes Shipwreck Society; Thunder Bay/North of Superior Tourism

CREATIVE SERVICES:
East Coast Studios, Merritt Island, Florida

EDITORIAL SERVICES:
Susan Albury

Library of Congress Cataloging-in-Publication Data

Beckett, Harry, 1936-
    Lake Superior / by Harry Beckett.
        p. cm. — (Great Lakes of North America)
    Includes bibliographical references and index.
    Summary: Discusses Lake Superior's geography, history, early inhabitants, important events, economy, and more.
        ISBN 0-86593-528-9
    1. Superior, Lake Juvenile literature. [1. Superior, Lake.] I. Title. II. Series: Beckett, Harry, 1936- Great Lakes of North America.
F552.B24 1999
977.4'9—dc21
                                                99-20529
                                                CIP

Printed in the USA

TABLE OF CONTENTS

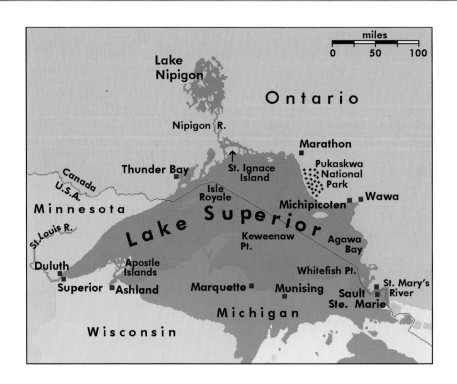

FACTS AND FIGURES FOR LAKE SUPERIOR

Length	350 miles	563 kilometers
Width	160 miles	257 kilometers
Average depth	483 feet	147 meters
Maximum depth	1,332 feet	406 meters
Volume	2,900 cubic miles	12,100 cubic kilometers
Water surface area	31,700 sq. miles	82,100 sq. kilometers
Shoreline (inc. islands)	2,726 miles	4,385 kilometers
Area of basin	49,300 sq. miles	127,700 sq. kilometers
Height above sea level	600 feet	183 meters
Retention time*	191 years	

* The average time that it takes for a molecule of water to enter and leave the lake.

ABOUT LAKE SUPERIOR

The French call the most northerly lake *Lac Supérieur*. It means the upper or top lake, but its English name suits it well. Lake Superior is the largest Great Lake in area and in volume of water. It is big enough to hold the water of all the other Great Lakes, and still leave room for three more Lake Eries. It holds one tenth of the world's surface freshwater, and it could flood North and South America to a depth of one foot.

Ontario lies to its north and east, Minnesota to its northwest, and Michigan and Wisconsin to its south. The Nipigon River flows southward from Lake Nipigon into the lake, and the Saint Louis River enters at Duluth-Superior, on the border of Minnesota and Wisconsin. There are many other smaller feeder rivers and streams. Every year, 2 feet (60 centimeters) of water enters the lake from rivers, and 2 1/2 feet (75 centimeters) as snow or rain. The lake is vast, cold, deep, and powerful.

The northern shore is rocky, with sheer cliffs rising in places to 1,000 feet (305 meters). Near Munising, Michigan, the **elements** (EH luh mints) have sculpted strange shapes in the multicolored sandstone cliffs of Pictured Rocks. Agawa Bay has one of the world's finest pebble beaches. The largest islands in the lake are the Apostle Islands (Wisconsin), Isle Royale (Michigan), and Saint Ignace and Michipicoten (Ontario). On the rugged southern shore, Keweenaw Peninsula and Whitefish Point pose a danger to shipping as they jut far out into the lake. The lake basin is heavily wooded Canadian Shield.

Pukaskwa National Park is typical of Canadian Shield shoreline.

Water flows out of Lake Superior into Lake Huron through the Saint Mary's River. Gates on the river control the amount of flow. An International Joint Commission has decided that the lake surface must not be more than 602 feet (183 meters) above sea level.

The rocky north shore of Lake Superior

NATIVE PEOPLES AND EARLY EXPLORERS

The forests around Lake Superior were home to the Ojibwa (also called Chippewa), who were hunters and gatherers. The forests provided meat and berries for food and skins for clothing and tents for the summer. They provided saplings and bark for winter homes. The Ojibwa made excellent canoes for travel, fishing, and harvesting wild rice, and snowshoes and toboggans for winter travel.

Although they traded furs with them, they did not become involved in wars between Europeans and other Indian nations. The Iroquois respected the Ojibwa strength and they left them in peace after destroying the Huron. The Ojibwa and two related nations, the Ottawa and the Menominee, made up the Council of the Three Fires.

To the south of the lake, the Menominee lived by fishing and gathering wild rice in the shallow waters. Their name means "wild rice gatherers." They harvested the rice by bending bunches of grass over the canoe, and beating the seed heads with wooden **flails** (FLAILZ). The grains collected in the bottom of the canoe.

Étienne Brulé was the first European to speak the languages of the Algonquin and the Huron and the first to reach Lake Huron along the Ottawa River. He was probably the first to visit Lake Superior in 1622. The French trappers, Pierre Esprit Radisson and Medart Chouart des Grosseilliers traveled the lake for a season (1659-1660) and showed how rich the area was by returning with a canoe full of furs. About the same time, Father Claude-Jean Allouez, a French missionary, mapped the whole lake.

An Ojibwa chief (Michipocoten Island) called Maydoc-Bame-Kinungee painted by Francis Kane.

Regular fur trading on the lake was started by Daniel Greysolon, also known as Sieur Duluth. The first traders used birchbark canoes and, later, double-ended York boats that could carry greater loads. When the fur trade died out about a hundred years later, boat design changed again to suit the growing fishing industry.

An assay shop tested the metal content of ore for early miners.

TOWNS AND CITIES

In 1970, the towns of Fort William and Port Arthur were joined to form Thunder Bay (population 113,946). It was named for the mythical Thunderbird. The Kaministikwia River has been the entrance to the Northwest from the lakes since before the beginning of the fur trade. It is also the gateway to the Saint Lawrence Waterway for goods and people coming from the West.

Across the bay to the east, Nanibijou, the Sleeping Giant, a huge rocky formation that is 984 feet (300 meters) high and 21 miles (33 kilometers) long, protects the harbor from the huge lake's storms.

Fort William and Port Arthur were rivals for trade and each still has its own downtown and its own ethnic population of Ukrainians, Italians, and Finns, as well as of Polish, Scandinavian, Slovakian, Greek, German, and Dutch communities. Lakehead University provides post-secondary education to the area.

Named after Sieur Duluth, Duluth (population 85,493) is a busy port at the mouth of the Saint Louis River, on land once the home of Sioux and Ojibwa. The town is built partly on a rocky bluff, 600 to 800 feet (180 to 240 meters) above the lake. A parkway along the heights gives a fine view of the lake and the town. Where the river empties into the lake, **silt** (SILT) has formed a 9-mile (14.4-kilometer) long land spit, called Park Point, parallel to the shore. Ships enter Duluth Harbor through a channel **dredged** (DREJD) through the spit and under a 230-foot (70-meter) high aerial lift bridge.

A marina at Thunder Bay. Some say they can see a giant asleep across the bay.

The city has a university, museums, an orchestra, and ballet and theater companies. The town of Superior lies across the river in Wisconsin. The Duluth-Superior harbor is an excellent natural port at the head of the Saint Lawrence Waterway. It is the second busiest port in the United States.

Other towns on the lake are Ashland, Wisconsin, and Marquette, Michigan.

The entrance to Duluth Harbor

WORKING AROUND THE LAKE

Fur trading was the first business in the Lake Superior region. The furs taken in the forests were brought down the waterways in small canoes. At the lake they were transferred into larger canoes for their journey to Montreal. These canoes would return, loaded with trade goods and provisions for the West.

Now, iron ore from the Mesabi Range of Minnesota, grain from the prairies on the north shore, and petroleum from the west arrive at Duluth, Thunder Bay, Marquette, or Two Harbors by rail, road, or pipeline. They are loaded onto ships that will carry them to the ports of the Saint Lawrence Waterway and to the rest of the world. These ships then load up for the journey back to Lake Superior. Ports that move goods onward are called **transshipment** (trans SHIP mint) ports.

The rocks of the Canadian Shield are rich in minerals such as iron ore, copper, silver, nickel, gold, and coal. Mining and transshipment became possible when the Sault Sainte Marie Canal was built to allow large cargo carriers to pass through the Saint Mary's River into Lake Superior from the lower lakes.

Logging is another major industry. The trees of the northern forest are best suited for pulp and paper production. Until the building of the railroads, the logs were towed over the lake as large floating rafts. Now they are made into pulp and paper in cities like Thunder Bay, and are carried by rail or shipped through the lake ports. But the largest cargo is grain.

Lighthouses make sailing on the lakes safer.

As the fur trade died out, the fishing industry grew, and is still important.

Manufacturing is also important in the communities around the lake. Fishing, hunting, and sightseeing attract many tourists. Recreational boating and scuba diving on the many wrecks in the cold, clear water are growing in popularity.

A ship passes through the Sault Sainte Marie locks.

DISASTERS AND MYSTERIES

The lakes have many stories about ghost ships. In 1902, the *Bannockburn*, a sturdy steel steamer, left Port Arthur with a load of wheat. The captain of the *Algonquin* saw her sail by as he passed Keweenaw Point in hazy weather. He looked away for only a short time but when he looked back, the *Bannockburn* had disappeared. She never arrived at Sault Sainte Marie and a full search found no trace of her or her crew.

A lifebelt washed ashore many months later. Months afterward, the story began to spread that an oar had been found with the word *Bannockburn* carved on it. Soon sailors began reporting sightings of a ghost ship, covered in ice, steaming through the gloom on its endless journey to the Sault Sainte Marie locks.

On November 10, 1975, the *Edmund Fitzgerald* was battling toward the Sault Sainte Marie locks with a fierce storm blowing from **astern** (uh STURN). It was sailing in the shelter of the northern shore and carrying iron ore. Another ore-carrier, the *Arthur M. Anderson*, was following a few miles behind and the two freighters were in radio contact until about 7:00 PM. The *Anderson* reported seeing a vessel approaching, and the *Edmund Fitzgerald*, which had lost its radar, acknowledged. It added, "We are holding our own." A short time later, the *Anderson* could see the lights of three ships 17 miles ahead, but not the lights of the *Edmund Fitzgerald*, which should have been eight miles closer. The ship had disappeared from view and from the radar screen.

The George M. Cox *ran aground on a calm day.*

A few fragments, including a battered lifeboat, were recovered later, but no crewmember was ever found. When the wreckage was located on the lake bed, the **bow** (BAU) section was upright in the mud. The stern was upside down some distance away. The huge ship had broken in two. There are theories about the sinking, but it is still an unsolved mystery.

The Edmund Fitzgerald

INTERESTING PLACES

Fort William was the world's largest fur trading post. It is in Thunder Bay at the geographical center of Canada. Every July, thousands of **voyageurs** (voy uh ZHUR), Native people, and North West Company employees came together for two weeks at the Great Rendezvous.

The trappers came with their canoes full of furs, taken during the winter, to sell and trade and to enjoy civilization for a short time, while the Nor'westers came to buy furs and sell trade goods and provisions brought from Montreal. The voyageurs and natives would camp outside the fort. The warehouses and the lodgings of the Montreal agents were inside the **palisade** (PAL uh sade). As the fur trade declined, the fort lost its importance and finally closed. The last original building was removed in 1902. Old Fort William has been reconstructed as it was in the Great Rendezvous days, 14 miles (22.5 kilometers) upriver from the original site. Costumed staff reenact the busy, noisy days at the fort, demonstrating trapping methods and **bartering** (BAHR tur ing) for provisions. Visitors can paddle a 36-foot (11 meter) birchbark canoe along the banks of the Kaministikwia River, just as the voyageurs did.

All along the Lake Superior shore there are tunnels in the rock where miners once dug for minerals. Like many mining and fishing settlements, they have been abandoned.

Petroglyphs painted by Native people on the Pictured Rocks.

Silver Islet, across the bay from Thunder Bay, is only 77 feet (24 meters) in diameter and 8 feet (2.5 meters) above the water level. When prospectors found silver on the islet, they dug tunnels deep into the rock. They even built a small town complete with docks and a lighthouse. Fighting the storms of Lake Superior was a terrible job, but before the mine was closed and the lake flooded the tunnel and won back the island, they had mined $3.2 million in silver.

The replica of Old Fort William, built upstream from the original site

GLOSSARY

astern (uh STURN) — towards the back (stern) of the boat

barter (BAHR tur) — to trade one thing for another without using money

bow (BAU) — the front part of a boat

dredge (DREJ) — to clean out or deepen the bottom of a harbor or channel

elements (EH luh mints) — the climate, rain, sleet, wind, and snow

flail (FLAIL) — an implement for separating grain from the stalk

palisade (PAL uh sade) — a high wooden protective fence

silt (SILT) — fine particles e.g. of sand, found on the bottom of a body of water

transshipment (trans SHIP mint) — receiving goods from one place and shipping them on to another place

voyageur (voy uh ZHUR) — the paddlers who transported goods by canoe along the lakes

Silver Islet was still being mined in 1921.

INDEX

FURTHER READING

You can find out more about the Great Lakes with these helpful books and web sites:

• R. Livesey and A.G. Smith. *The Fur Traders,* Stoddart
• J. Lunn and C. Moore. *The Story of Canada,* Lester Publishing
• J. Lunn and C. Moore. *Native Peoples,* Lester Publishing
• A. J. Ray. *I have lived here since the world began,* Lester Publishing
• G. Legay. *Atlas of Indians of North America,* Barron's
• *Canada's Visual History CD Rom National Film Board of Canada*

• Great Lakes Information Network: www.great-lakes.net
• University of Minnesota Sea Grant: www.d.emn.edu/seagr/tourism.html
• www.ci.duluth.mn.us/city/mayor
• www.sundialnw.com_
• www.cciw.ca/glimr/geographic-search/superior/intra.html
• Quizzes on Lakes: ww.hebe.edu.on.ca/coll/lakes.htm